# Look at a Calf

## Dare Wright

Random House  New York

*With thanks to*
*the McNees of* BIDE-A-WEE *Farm,*
*and all the other Delaware County people*
*who helped with this book—*
*the Brydens of Chambers Hollow,*
*the Geers of Pines Brook,*
*the Kellys of Launt Hollow,*
*and the Taylors of Third Brook.*

Published in the United States by Random House, Inc., New York, and simultaneously in Canada by Random House of Canada Limited, Toronto.

*Library of Congress Cataloging in Publication Data*

Wright, Dare.

Look at a calf.

SUMMARY. Text and photographs introduce the characteristics of dairy cows and their calves and the dairy farming industry.

1. Dairying—Juvenile literature.    2. Calves—Juvenile literature.    [1. Dairying. 2. Cows]    I. Title.
SF239.5.W74    636.2'1'4    73-17369    ISBN 0-394-82776-7    ISBN 0-394-92776-1 (lib. bdg.)

Manufactured in the United States of America

Do you drink milk?
Calves do.
A calf is a cow's baby.

A calf grows inside the cow for nine months. Then it is big enough to come into the world. This calf was born in the farm pasture. The mother cow licked and nudged her wet baby.

Within half an hour the calf was standing up on long, wobbly legs and looking around for her first meal. It was ready for her. The cow's baglike udder was full of milk.

Before the calf could begin sucking the cow's milk, the farmer came. He carried the baby off to the barn, where he could take the best care of her. Her mother called after her, "Moo-moo-oo."

The farmer put the calf in a clean, dry stall. He fed her milk. Already she could drink from a bottle or a bucket.

At first she must have milk that comes from her own mother or another cow who has just had a calf. This milk has special things in it to protect the calf from sickness. After four days she can drink milk from any cow in the herd, and start on hay and grain. Hay is dried grasses, clover, and other plants. Grain is the seeds of cereal plants like wheat and oats.

If a calf stays in the pasture with the cow, she drinks all the milk she needs right from her mother's udder, and eats the growing grass. She may nurse for as long as nine months.

In the barn, the farmer weans the calf when she is between one and three months old. She doesn't need milk
anymore. From now on she can eat like a grown cow.

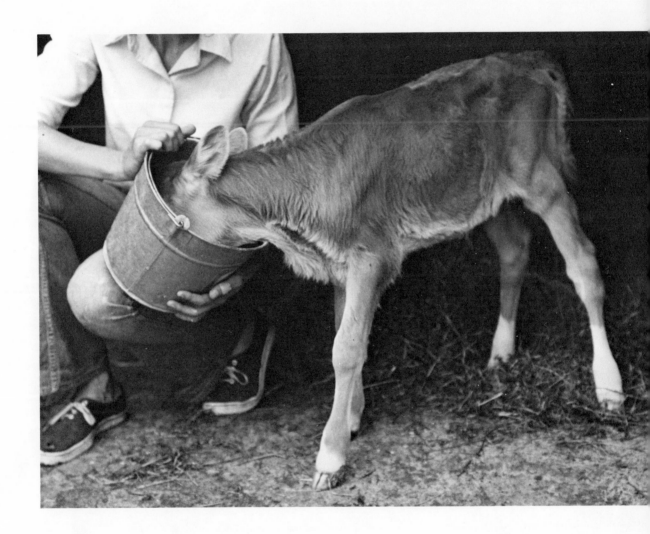

Cows make milk to feed their own babies, but
they make more than one small calf needs. The
farmer milks the cows, and sells the extra milk for
people to use.

A female calf grows up to be a cow.

This cow is one of a special kind that gives more milk than other cows. She is a dairy cow. She lives on a farm, and the farmer takes good care of her.

In the summer she grazes in the green fields. In the winter she stays in the warm barn.

Full-grown cows should have horns like these, but many farmers stop the horns from growing. They put a de-horning paste or liquid on the calf's head where the horns would sprout. They don't want their cows to scratch or hurt each other by accident.

A wild cow needs horns to protect herself and her calf, but a dairy cow has a safe home.

A male calf grows into a bull. Bulls aren't good-natured like cows. They get angry easily, and can be dangerous. A farmer puts a ring in the bull's nose so he can control and lead him without being harmed.

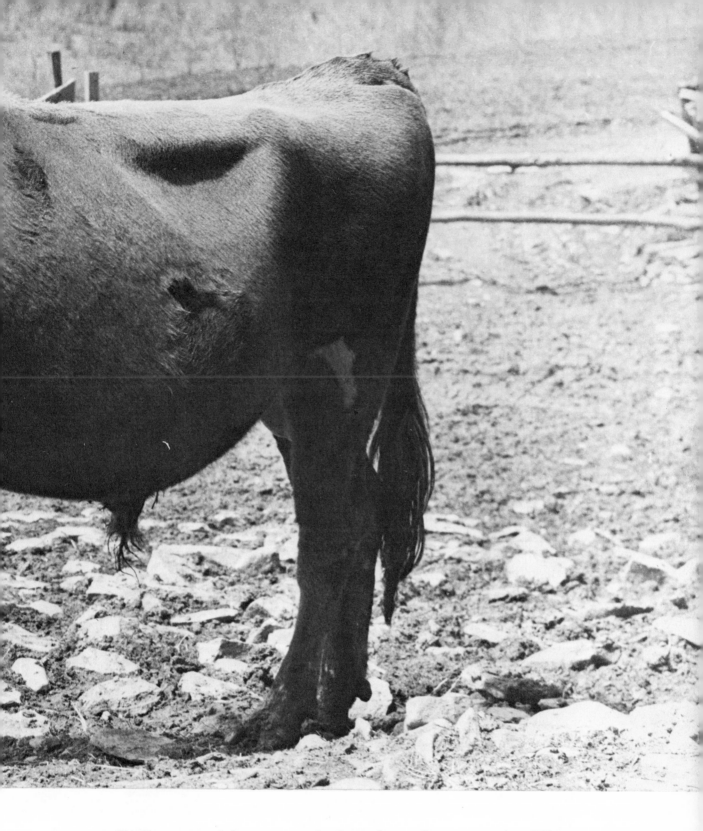

Bulls are bigger and heavier than cows. They don't give milk. They are fathers. Without them there wouldn't be any calves. Then the cows wouldn't make any milk, and people wouldn't get a share of it.

The cow was one of the first animals tamed by human beings.

No one knows how many thousands of years cattle have been serving people. They are mentioned in the oldest writings. They are shown in the oldest pictures.

Early men used cattle in many ways. They ate their meat and drank their milk. They made leather from their skins. Cattle pulled plows and carts. They carried people and burdens on their backs.

Sometimes cows took the place of money. Wealth wasn't added up in gold or dollars, but in cows. A man could buy a wife with a cow.

There are places where people still use cows in all these ways. No cow is more useful in more places than the dairy cow.

There are different breeds of dairy cows. The best known are the Holsteins, Jerseys, Guernseys, Ayrshires, and Brown Swiss.

Dairy cows aren't all the same color. They can be plain or spotted. They can be white, black, grey, red, fawn, brown, or a mixture of these colors.

This calf is a Jersey.

Jerseys are pale grey, or fawn, or dark brown. They have big eyes and long eyelashes.

Jerseys first came to America on the early sailing ships. A sailing ship took weeks and weeks to cross the Atlantic Ocean. There were no refrigerators then to keep milk fresh on the long voyage. But the cows on board gave fresh milk every day.

A week-old Jersey like this one weighs about 50 pounds. A one-year-old weighs 450 to 500 pounds. A grown-up Jersey cow weighs between 900 and 1000 pounds. That's not very heavy for a cow. There are much bigger breeds that give more milk, but a Jersey gives the richest and creamiest milk of all.

A cow doesn't have any milk until her first calf is born. She can bear a calf when she's two years old, and then have one every year.

The farmer milks the cow for ten months after her calf is born. Then he stops for two months while she "dries off" and waits for her next calf. When the calf arrives, her milk will come again.

A nine-month-old calf isn't a cow yet, and doesn't graze with the herd. But she's growing fast.

She's a year old now. She's called a heifer. She's
turned out to pasture with the grown-up cows.

Cows spend a lot of their lives eating, as much as eight hours a day.

Cows' teeth are arranged differently from people's. At the sides, cows have strong teeth top and bottom to grind up their food. In the front they have teeth only at the bottom. Instead of top teeth, there's a tough pad of skin. Cows wind their tongues around the grass and plants, and tear this growing food off against the pad.

Cows have four stomachs to break down all the rough stems and leaves they eat. Even when they're not eating, they chew a lot—because cows don't swallow their food just once. They chew a mouthful until it's damp enough to get down. The food begins to soften in the first and second stomachs. Then the cow coughs it up in a ball to chew again. This is called chewing a cud.

Cows do it all day long—chew and swallow, cough up, chew, and swallow again. At last this continuous meal is swallowed for good, and is digested by all four stomachs.

A Jersey cow eats about six tons of food a year. That's 12,000 pounds.

In return for all the grass, hay, grain, and other things the farmer feeds her, the Jersey cow can give 10,000 pounds of milk a year.

Cows also make a lot of manure. Every day the farmer takes the manure and spreads it on the croplands and the pastures to help grow more food.

Cows whisk their tails and scratch a lot to get rid of the flies that pester them.

They lie down to rest in the heat of the day
while they chew and chew on their cuds.

Morning and evening, cows come in from the fields to be milked. They are creatures of habit, and they know when milking time is near. They wait at the gate until the farmer lets them into the barn.

The farmer is careful to handle the cows the same way every day. He always milks at the same time. Any change in routine might upset the cows, and then they wouldn't give all their milk.

Each cow knows her own place in the barn. If the farmer shifts even one cow, the whole herd will get mixed up. The cows' heads are fastened between wooden bars, called stanchions, which keep them in their stalls.

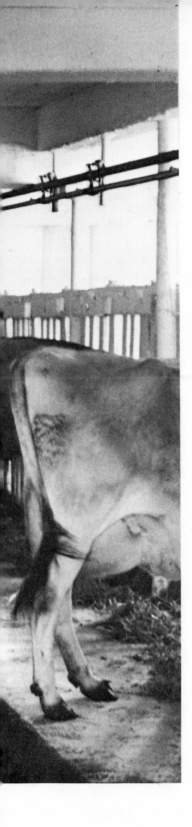

The cows have to stay in one place, but they can move a little, eat, and lie down. Behind them is a gutter to catch their manure. Everything in the barn is kept very clean so the milk you buy will be clean, too.

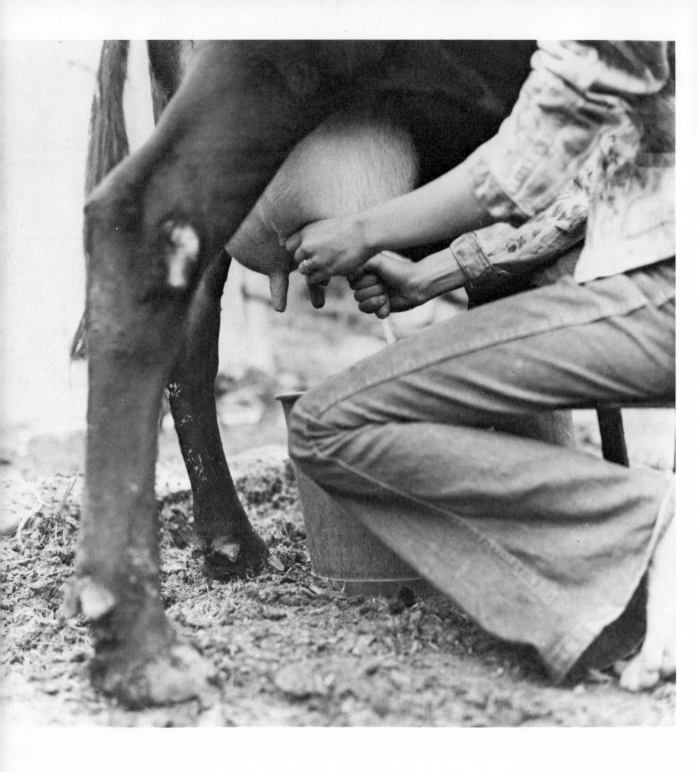

This is the way cows were milked for thousands
of years. A person can draw out the milk by hand
just as well as a calf can suck it out. A hand-milker
can milk from six to twelve cows an hour.

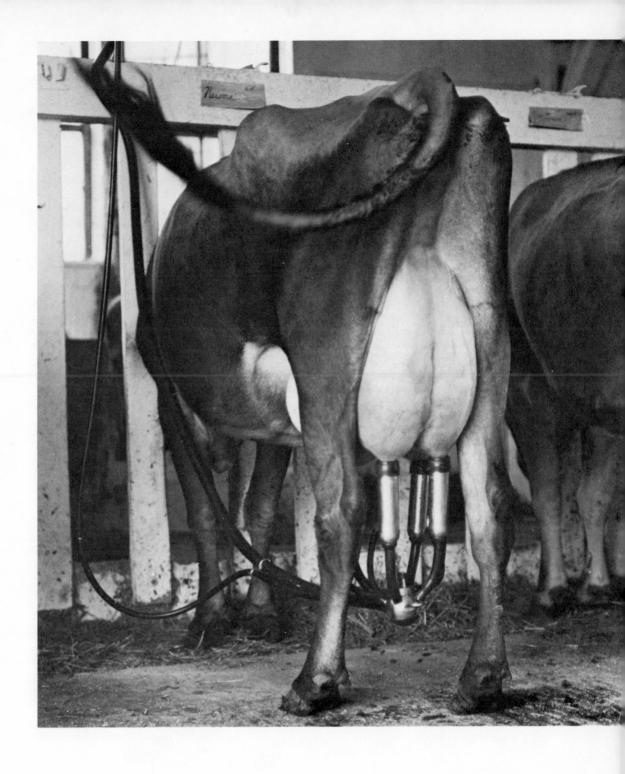

This is the way most cows are milked today—by
a machine. The milking machine sucks the milk out
into pipes that carry it away to a storage tank. A
machine can milk more cows in less time.

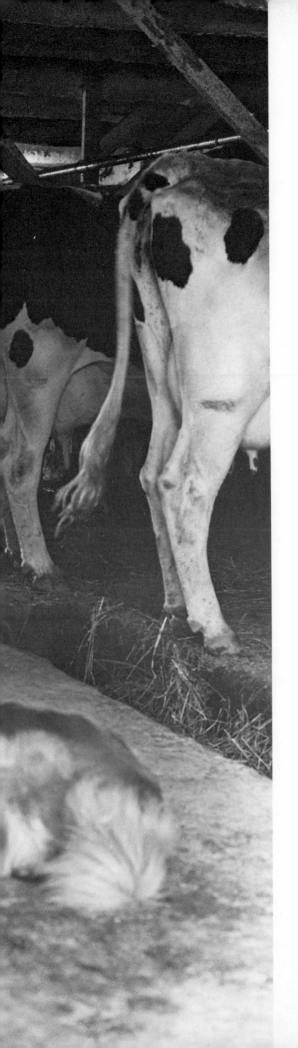

There are still small farms on the hills and in the valleys where you can see things done the old ways.

The sunlight falls through the open door.

The cows wait patiently for the farmer with his milking stool and pail.

The farm dog dozes in the warm light and the warm smells.

The barn cats lap up their bowl of new milk.

All this may soon be gone.

Today the world needs so much milk that dairy farming is a great industry. People keep thinking up new methods and new machines to get more milk faster.

This is one way of getting more milk faster.

In a special building called a milking parlor, just one or two people can milk between fifty and one hundred cows an hour.

The cows enter this milking parlor six at a time.

The milkers stand in a pit on a level with the cows' udders. The milking machines go on, and the foaming, white milk flows into a row of glass tanks. Then the six cows go out through the front doors, and six more come in through the back doors, like cars on the assembly line.

From the glass tanks the milk flows through more pipes into a big refrigerated tank, where it stays cold and clean.

About every two days, a huge tank truck comes to
the farms, picks up the milk, and takes it to dairy plants.

The dairy plants get the milk ready to be shipped to
stores in towns and cities. Then people can buy it.

Calves like milk. Cats like milk. Children like milk, and lots of things that are made from milk.

Butter, cheese, sour cream, yogurt, and ice cream
are some of the foods that are made from milk.

Milk from cows helps to feed people all over the world. But cows don't make their milk for people. They make it for their calves.